# In the Dark

Written by Emma Lynch

It is dark in the town.

The lights are off.

Look at the moon and the bright stars.

They are as bright as a torch.

owl

fox

The night is still. It is cool and moist.

bat

moth

Now the nocturnal animals
start to prowl.

Nocturnal animals sleep in the light.

They hunt for food in the dark.

Owls can see well in the dark.

They sit in trees, then swoop
down to hunt.

A fox lurks next to the bins.
She looks for food for her cubs.

She avoids the town in the light.

Bats dart across the gardens.
They can not see well.

They wait for insect noises,
then swoop to grab them.

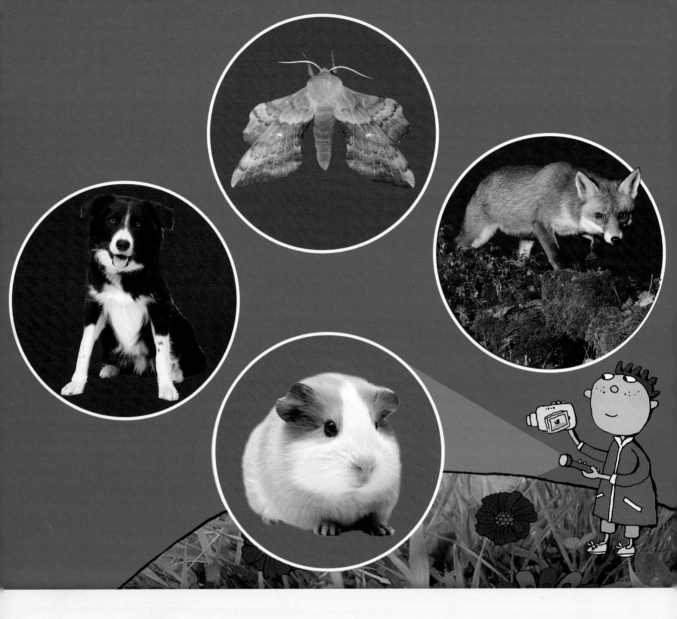

Can you spot the nocturnal animals?